Looking for Matthew

Matthew Avery Solomon
March 3, 1985 – September 4, 2008

Looking for Matthew

Poems by Bill Denham

the apocryphile press
BERKELEY, CA
www.apocryphile.org

apocryphile press
BERKELEY, CA

Apocryphile Press
1700 Shattuck Ave #81
Berkeley, CA 94709
www.apocryphile.org

Printed in the United States of America
ISBN 978-1-937002-69-5

This book is dedicated to Jayvion and to Makai—
that they may know this part of their story.

a personal journey . . .

Sometimes I simply sob,
    not knowing, even, the trigger
    that loosed the flood,
    that swept me
    into that maelstrom—
    feeling wracked,
    stretched too taut
    to bear another second.

And as these feelings pass,
    and my shoulders
    know the calm,
    sometimes I can begin
    to trace my tears
    to this or that
    unwelcomed loss
    of which my life
    has been too full.

And who can say
    the cause of that?
    Or the blessings
    held there-in?

Oh, the freedom
    to weep
    is hard
    won.

Foreword

My heart went cold that September morning when the voice on my cell phone identified herself as an SFPD Homicide Detective. I knew Matthew was dead.

Yet even as I felt the numbness come over me and knew the rage and sorrow that were to come—I am no stranger to loss—I knew a far greater grief, beyond the personal, a profound sadness for the lives of the two young men who murdered Matthew—two young men who must live without hope, like thousands of others, who see no future for themselves and have little regard for life—their own or another's.

Matt's short life followed a different arc.

Though he had good reason to despair, though he did struggle and make serious mistakes, he never gave up. He was given away by his biological mother at the age of three—a conscious, painful memory for him—and adopted by a family who, despite good intentions, added further to his trauma. And he did act out during his teenage years. At seventeen he helped his older brother commit an armed robbery. Two years later he turned himself in to the authorities and served eighteen months in San Quentin State Prison.

Not everyone would do that. He had begun to grow up.

Matt was a poet. He had been writing and making poems since Middle School, when a large poster of Tupac hung above his bed.

In those days we hung out, shot hoops each afternoon and I listened to his poems in the evening after dinner. In prison he took a writing course. Encouraged by his instructor, he wrote poignantly of prison life and his own internal struggles. "Keep at it," she told him. And he did.

On Saturday night October 15, 2005 he shared the stage with several other spoken word artists, three times his age—myself, Maya Spector and Doug Von Koss—in the old, craftsman sanctuary at Grace North Church in Berkeley and movingly spoke his rap poem, *Love*, to an attentive audience. The poem, written behind prison bars, is lost, now, along with all his notebooks—taken by vandals after his death.

We loved the spoken word, Matt and I, and he encouraged me to bring my poems to the open mic and join him at The Starry Plough. I never did. But I do make poems like his—poems to be spoken—brought to life by the sounds and rhythms of the human voice. So it is with these poems, born from my grief and spoken aloud, that I honor our common love and his short life.

I knew Matthew for twenty of his twenty-three years. I was part of his complex extended family and assumed a parental role frequently with him and the other children. Growing up he called me Uncle Bill. I speak of him now as my stepson, for his adopted family had disintegrated by his early adolescence and by the time he got out of prison, I was the only parental figure he could call upon. He came to live with me for a year when he got out of San Quentin. The homicide detective found my name and phone number on his emergency card, in his wallet.

Bill Denham
Oakland, California

The early days . . .

The *Day* number indicates the day of creation, the number of days since Matthew's death. The opening poem above came on *Day 85*.

Day 2

Matt

You made choices—
    but your options were limited
    by our failures, the adults in your life
    who were charged with your care.
    I will not catalog those failures.
    That is for each of us to do
    if we so choose
    but I will risk saying publicly
    what I have said to you
    in private—'For our collective failures,
    I am so, so sorry.'
    May you rest in peace.

The emerald flash

We stood on the deck together at the end of the day,
    high up the hillside in Pacifica, facing the Farallones,
    this young adolescent boy and me—quietly
    watching the sun slip into the sea,
    hoping to catch that rarest of moments,
    the emerald flash. And there it was!
    Astonishing! Brilliant! The fire red sun
    turned green—hardly a second—
    then gone!

Nearly ten years on, now, from that day
    and three more away from a muzzle flash,
    I wake in the pre-dawn dark
    and know a fleeting moment of grace—
    oh, blessèd moment of grace—
    before the terrible weight descends.
    Matt is dead! Gone in a flash!
    And I pulled the trigger,
    stole his warmth,
    laid his body out cold and stiff
    on the coroner's table—
    a liminal image
    frozen now,
    forever,
    in my
    mind.

Oh, how I know the truth of that—
        how I am alive, how Matt is dead.
        My boy is dead! He is my boy, yes!
        Though we shared not a single gene,
        his death is my weight to carry.

I hear your doubts, your wish to comfort
        but hold your tongue and listen.
        Do not tell me I did the best I could,
        for I know the story, the whole story.
        Yes, we had spoken truth to one another.
        We had connected, healed to some degree,
        but blowback is forever
        and in the end, our time too short
        our efforts not enough.
        And here I am alive, my boy is dead.
        I am the adult, he was the child—
        this one is on me.

Yes, we saw that emerald flash together.
        Not knowing what made the fire go green
        nor how the end things would come,
        we loved the joy of beauty shared.
        And I hold that moment,
        as I hold Matt's body, cold,
        laid out on the coroner's table
        and know I have no time left
        to *try* to love myself.
        And I don't need to tell you
        how painful and how hard
        this work of love is!

Day 5

Hope

Death ends the hope a life can give.
  Matt's gone. What might have been
  for him or us is gone.
  Yet hope lives in a beating heart,
  even one as cold as Cain's
  who spilled his brother's blood
  and walks beneath its weight.

I feel that weight as if it were my own.
  It is my own!
  Where do I turn, then,
  when these acts of despair,
  are raised up all 'round me
  as tests of manhood,
  as tickets of acceptance?
  How am I to judge myself
  in this world?
  What is my measure?
  What am I to do?
  How do I assume
  responsibility?
  Tell me!

How are we to take it, collectively?
    How are we to end complicity?
    How are we to manifest hope
    that might touch a young man,
    who lives without it,
    might save another Matthew
    or save his nameless assassin?
    Tell me!

Let me know! Let me know
    how you live in this world,
    how you hold hope,
    how you tell your story
    to your neighbors,
    to your brothers and sisters,
    sons and daughters?
    Let me know! I'll be here
    stumbling along.
    Come find me,
    let me know!

Day 9

Matt's funeral

You know what I hate about funerals?
    Well, there are lots of things
    but I'll start with preachers
    who think they can offer consolation
    by slamming Islam, Judaism and Buddhism,
    as if that had anything to do with Matthew.

I console myself, by remembering Matthew,
    which is what everybody else was doing there
    and the stories were all the same,
    all two hours of them, coming from white people,
    black people, brown people, well-off people,
    poor people on the edge,
    ex-cons and homies, work buddies,
    sisters-in-law and aunties—
    not officially, not legally, understand,
    for Matt didn't marry Hazel or Hakiti
    the mothers of Jayvion and Makai.
    But that didn't matter—not here, not now.

And some of those stories were more real,
    more honest, than others,
    but nobody was like the preacher—
    even the auntie, who was struggling
    with her grief by talking Jesus talk.

She was hurting, no hiding that,
    and felt that terrible loss of connection.
    That's what all the stories were about—connection.
    Everyone there felt connected to Matthew.

There was no more beautiful smile in the universe
    than Matt's smile—once you saw that smile
    you were done, it was over, he was in your heart
    and that smile came from inside, from somewhere real
    and that smile was on the face of a young man
    who had been dealt a crummy hand.

I know. I know the whole story.
    And it was inspirational to hear each person
    speak of how Matt had touched their lives,
    and how they had born witness to all his efforts
    to turn his life around and to his love
    for Jayvion and Makai.
    I know the back story,
    the parts they didn't say
    and that's ok. I'll give them that.
    It wasn't a white wash. It was real
    and I knew, as I listen, me and Matt, we're alike,
    the way that works with your children, sometimes—
    when we can see ourselves in them and them in us
    and sometimes that's a joy,
    sometimes a sadness,
    a cause for grief.

But Matt . . . Matt was hope
    in the midst of hopelessness.
    He was smiling and laughing
    with his friends when he was shot,
    from behind—one bullet to the head, one to the back—
    by two masked kids in an act of retaliation
    or initiation—who knows what?
    Maybe some kind of turf war,
    right here, not halfway 'round the world
    in Afghanistan or Iraq—right here.

So when I spoke of Matt, that evening, I spoke of that hope,
    but you should know I only said a part
    of what was on my mind—the other part,
    the part I played in his upbringing—those mistakes,
    the owning of which allowed for hope
    but could not erase, in so short a time, if ever,
    the limits laid down on the life of this child—
    I carried that part with me as I left the mortuary
    with my son, Leslie, and his friend.
    It went unspoken
    but I carry it and I will carry it
    each minute of every day.
    What I do with that is on me.
    There is no helping Matthew.
    There's only remembering him.

Day 10

Thank you

"after funerals we are saying thank you"
W.S. Merwin

For years I was deceived
    or more truthfully,
    deceived myself
    into believing
    what I saw
    before me
    was other
    than it
    was.

And the harm that
    has come
    to others
    from my
    self-deception
    is greater
    than any
    words
    can
    ever
    say.

Yet, through my tears,
    I do say,
    Thank
    you.

Day 16

My grief's companion

My deeply rich, purple-blue delphinium
    sprang up beside the brown stalk
    of its mother, whose flowers
    had long ago dropped their petals
    to the grass—sprang up unannounced,
    as if it knew my need or hers.

And this new gift,
    this off-spring of its mother's roots,
    stretched up and up and up again,
    well beyond her height,
    (as Matt had done with Mary)
    and even well above my own,
    and slowly with each new opening bud,
    became a giant cone of color,
    cradled, at its base, by three smaller ones,
    who seemed to gesture in deference,
    drooping low beneath the weight
    of their own flowers.

And now these petals begin to drop away,
    my grief's companion, passing, too,
    more slowly and more naturally
    than Matt was allowed to do.
    That bullet to his brain,
    dropped him, mid-smile,
    to the ground
    and though you may argue
    children killing children
    is but a part of human nature
    (remember Cain?)
    and no different, in the end,
    from my delphinium's passing,
    death is death, after all,
    and all things that live must die.
    I will grant you that
    but say and know in my heart
    that Matt had only just begun to bloom.
    And there's my grief,
    assuaged a moment
    by the beauty
    of my flower.

Day 16

December's eyes

Her ears ringing from the shots,
    she could not hear herself scream,
    "They shot Matt and Noel!
    They shot Matt and Noel!"

People turned from the bar,
    looked up from their conversations,
    as if they could not understand
    what they saw and heard—
    this young woman
    standing in the doorway,
    calling for help,
    not knowing she, too, had been shot,
    blood flowing down her arm,
    her sweatshirt clinging
    to her flesh—
    or perhaps they did know,
    all too well, what they saw
    and did not or could not move.

She tracked their eyes, looked down at her arm,
    turned and ran back to her friends
    who lay in pools of blood—
    Matt dead, Noel dying as police arrived.
    They told her Matt was dead, tended to Noel,
    and loaded the two of them and Matt's body
    into the ambulance.

Noel died, too,
    but December, that was her name,
    lived to tell the story,
    the three of them hanging out after work—
    Noel doing his karaoke thing
    while she and Matt cracked up.
    She spoke of their decision
    to cruise the street when the next act up
    was a country western.
    They were just hanging out, being friends,
    walking back and forth a bit
    when she sat down on a Muni bench—
    the three of them, joking and playing around,
    helping each other that way,
    never suspecting a thing.
    Then the shots rang out—and it was done.

Two masked gunmen, she was told,
    got in a van and drove away.
    She never saw them.
    But her eyes, now, her beautiful eyes,
    have a look that's hard to hold—
    not glazed over, not shut down.
    They're simply eyes that know,
    know exactly what they have seen.

On being left behind

There is an isolation in death,
   in being left behind
   in a sea of grief
   and going down,
   unable to breathe the air
   the other's life had brought,
   as if you were looking up
   through the waves' refracted light,
   where distorted and insubstantial faces,
   gestures, words seem tossed about,
   seem to float along the surface,
   somewhere up there, above you—
   words and gestures from friends who care,
   who know and feel your loss,
   who, no doubt, have known their own
   and wish to pull you back
   to help you breathe again
   the air connection gives.

   And though you may know
   you will not drown,
   you feel the isolation
   of being left
   behind.

On the death of a child

To lose a child
    is to close in
    on the loss of hope.

A dangerous time, this,
    for in our flailing, our crying out,
    finding ourselves sucked down
    by this maelstrom of grief,
    we easily move toward self deception,
    speak untruths to ourselves,
    to keep our pain at bay.
    Should we do so,
    deny our grief,
    we lose ourselves.
    And in that loss
    we lose hope.

Looking for Matthew

He's gone . . . he is gone . . .
    but we must look for Matthew.
    We must look for Matt
    where we can find him—
    in Jayvion and Makai, of course,
    in that genetic and physical kind of way,
    but in ourselves, as well,
    in that way that you are another me
    and I am another you,
    and there, in that place,
    I see myself in Matt
    and Matt in me
    and not just in the smile,
    the determination,
    the vision of what might be,
    for Matt and I
    shared all that
    but shared, as well, much more—
    the struggles, the darker side
    that sometimes brought us low
    but never held us there.

So I look for Matt each day,
   where, now, he lives—
   inside of me and I say,
   "Whassssup bro?"
   and he gives me
   that look of his—
   a gift, in my mind's eye,
   that'll carry me,
   carry me through
   another day.
   It's all I
   can do
   but still
   I hurt,
   still I
   cry.

This I believe

I hear the voice of fear
    and I am afraid.
    I hear the voice of hope
    and I have hope.
    I hear the silence of the voiceless,
    and I weep—
    for I know that silence
    is shattered time and again,
    time and again by the sound of shots—
    and my child, *our child,*
    lies dead on the street,
    my street, *our street*
    and I weep, I weep
    for that loss
    of hope.

Yet, I live. I breathe and I speak
    and though I weep
    and though I am afraid
    and lie awake in the dark of night,
    I must not be silent.
    My voice, quavering
    as it sometimes may be,
    must speak the certainty I know,
    must be a voice for the voiceless,
    must be a voice of hope.
    This I believe.

Day 53

Matt's ashes

I cannot track the days.
    Maybe it's been a week, maybe more
    since we laid Matthew's ashes to rest—
    what was left of him,
    placed in a small, burnished-brass box,
    unadorned but for a tiny brass plaque,
    that named the name, told the dates
    above a single, short statement:

    Matt's life was a life of hope.

And where is that hope, now?
    It must be in Jayvion and Makai
    for children are our hope,
    their eyes so clear—look!
    Look into their eyes,
    then know, with certainty,
    not a hint of doubt,
    that the hope we see there,
    must be a reflection of our own.
    Though our aging eyes weep
    from the suffering, injustice and hopelessness
    we feel and see around us,
    we must hold fiercely to the knowledge
    that for our children, hope lives in us.

Certainly, our only task on this earth
    is to nurture the hope in these eyes,
    in the souls of our children—
    and make no mistake,
    they are all our children,
    our responsibility,
    and our hope.

On the day we gathered at the crematorium—
    Hazel with Jayvion and Anthony,
    Hakiti with Makai and her own mom,
    Uncle Harold and myself—
    each struggling in our own way,
    at once, together and alone,
    little two year old Makai
    spilled his cup of water
    on the coffee table.
    Still thirsty, looking square
    into his mother's young eyes
    as she sat leaning forward on the sofa,
    holding all that she was holding—inside,
    he raised both his small hands,
    ever so softly, ever so gently
    in a Matthew kind of way,
    held her face between them,
    and in a voice, clear and trusting as his eyes,
    asked her for more water.

Later, after the ashes had been placed
    in the columbarium, we sat in silence.
    Makai's eyes sparkled like his dad's
    but lacked the weight of knowledge
    that shown through the light
    in his older brother's eyes
    on this day, in this place,
    where the ashes of their father lay.
    Anthony, Jayvion's small half-brother,
    like Makai, early in his third year, was restless.
    He walked toward Makai,
    who stood facing the glass covered alcove
    that housed his father's ashes.
    Reaching out with curiosity
    and the same gentleness
    Makai had shown,
    he lightly touched
    his hair—his beautifully curly,
    Tongan, African,
    haole hair.

Day 94

Matthew's gift

In that time . . .
    approaching my sixtieth year,
    or maybe just past it,
    when I had begun opening
    a door here and another there, into my soul,
    I came upon one, almost by accident,
    for it was nearly hidden from my view
    in a dark corner, far from the light,
    where dark loving vines, large from age
    and thick with new growth,
    had all but covered it.
    And with great effort,
    I managed to pry it open
    and caught a momentary
    vision of what had been
    hidden from me
    for all those years
    of unshed tears.

And I thought, to myself,
    in that mistaken way we do
    when first we manage
    to pry such doors ajar,
    "Oh . . . this will be
    my year to grieve."

And, now, closing rapidly
    on my seventieth year,
    moving, it seems, ever more slowly,
    with each new day speeding by,
    a smaller part of the whole,
    I have found a way to weep—
    a gift from Matthew
    that he may never know
    his death gave to me
    and, finally, I am here,
    ready to accept my tears,
    ready to weep.

And I do. They come, now,
    as if they had a will of their own,
    which is true of tears.
    They come when they want to,
    when *they* need to be wept,
    when they *need* to be wept,
    for me or for another.

Oh . . . I have looked into that abyss that is me
    and I weep. I am free,
    now, to weep.

And two years on . . .

One right action

There is but one right action in response to the death of a child—
    to live one's life as fully and deeply as possible,
    engaging every moment,
    working when it's time to work,
    weeping when it's time to weep,
    dancing when it's time to dance,
    holding nothing back,
    so when our time is up,
    we will have left it
    all on the ground
    and be ready.

In this way we honor the life too early snuffed out.

Grief

Grief felt, grief embraced
    is the handmaid to beauty—
    a rich living soil
    that brings the soul to flower
    and then to fruit and then to harvest
    in daily acts of compassion,
    which is to say justice,
    which is to say beauty.

Grief ignored, grief buried
    is the handmaid to hate—
    a sterile, despoiled soil
    that stunts the growing soul,
    twists and turns it in upon itself,
    withers it away
    in daily acts of fear,
    which is to say injustice,
    which is to say hate.

O, Felix culpa! Oh, light from Darkness!

In a split second,
    as is always the case,
    even as internal growth
    creeps as slowly
    as deep time, itself,
    my life changed forever
    and stayed, as well,
    more deeply
    the same.

A masked young man,
    a gun in hand,
    pointed at the back
    of Matthew's head—close in,
    chose in that split second
    to move his index finger
    hardly half an inch—
    once, twice, three times more
    and in that small act
    became executioner.
    Matthew lay dead on the street.
    Noel, his buddy, lay fatally bleeding.

How is it, then,
    I pulled the trigger?
    That is the only question.
    And the only answer I know
    is the story of my life,
    the story of Matthew's life,
    the story of Noel's life,
    the story of this nameless young assassin's life.
    For, in fact, we are all in this together.
    We are inexorably one with the other.
    That's just the way it is—
    always the way it is.

I know nothing
    of the executioner,
    nearly nothing of Noel,
    save the profound agony
    I saw in his immigrant parents' eyes.
    I do know something of Matthew—
    for twenty of his twenty-three years
    I was in his life and formed it
    in whatever ways I did—
    for good or for ill.

But mostly I know myself—
    more honestly, I try to
    and this nameless young man
    forced upon me, in that split second,
    no doubt, thoughtlessly,
    the need for me to see
    myself as executioner—
    all those tiny
    infinitesimal
    acts that
    kill.

O, Felix culpa! Oh, light from darkness!

Employee of the Month – Goodwill Industries San Francisco, August 2008.

*But Matt . . . Matt was hope
in the midst of hopelessness.*

Afterword

I share these moments, in the manner of Matthew, by which I mean spoken words from my heart, to honor his time among us that lives in our memory, to make concrete in this way, the hope he manifested in a life, too short.

The voice is mine, the experiences mine. The words, like Matt's, come as spoken words and are meant to be spoken and heard. Clearly, I have not told you everything. You need not know everything to know and feel the individual and the broader tragedy of this story and the hope that emanates from it.

May it now become a part of you, in the way of stories and so keep Matt's gentle spirit among us.

Bill Denham

Acknowledgements

The words are mine but they owe their existence to the many people who have touched my life—my teachers, all—my family, my children, the mothers of my children, my dear friends—the lovers of language whose poems I have read and heard spoken and taken to heart and committed to memory—the community of men surrounding the Redwood Men's Center and the singers of the Noah Project who first inspired me to speak and to transcribe the words of my heart and who have held and born witness to my life ever since and Robert Johnson whose wisdom and gentle blessing moves me still and whose concept of one right action guides my footsteps and my dear friend Sean Morris who first brought me into this remarkable circle and whose friendship surpasses words.

In the preparation of this book, I have been helped by the skilled eyes and wisdom of fellow printers and book artists: Yvonne Tsang, Kim Vanderheiden, Richard Seibert and Mary Laird, Marie Dern and Joan Downs. This book could have never come into existence without the creative and supportive and fun-loving environment at Painted Tongue Press in Oakland, California, and all the people who make it and have made it so over the years—especially Bettina Pauly and Mitsuko Baum. And John Mabry of Apocryphile Press did everything that was necessary to publish the book in paperback. I owe a large debt of gratitude to each of these artists, craftspeople, and entrepreneurs.

The images of sandhill cranes in flight are from a photograph taken by Bill Denham at Paynes Prairie State Reserve, South of Gainesville, Florida in December 2003. The reversed photograph was turned to silhouette by Tamara Gronet of Studio G.

The line drawing of Matthew's face was done by his brother, Leslie Denham-Newman, on September 6, 2008.

The photograph of Matthew was provided by Deborah Alverez-Rodriguez of Goodwill Indrustries, San Francisco, California.

SF Chronicle 9/6/2008 ▪ Spate of killings roils Mission District
http://www.sfgate.com/bayarea/article/Spate-of-killings-roils-Mission-District-3196368.php

The publication of this book has been generously supported by grants from
John and Julia Denham & Bob and Rachel Denham

and on Indiegogo by over one hundred individuals and couples, including:

Richard and Naomi Applebaum, Pam and Al Bendich,
Leslie Denham, John Solomon, Maurice Wren,
Michael Blacksburg, June and Newt Smith,
June Quackenbush Hartung, Barbara Hazard,
Kim Vanderheiden, Adrian Bozzolo, Ken Solomon,
Howard Curtis, Mary Austin, Sean and Jen Morris,
Karen Difrummolo, Scott and Cathy Denham,
John Christenson, Jim and Joyce Glann,
Richard and Lindzi Mapplebeck-Palmer,
Dennis Peterson, Laura Rolen, Andy Riffle

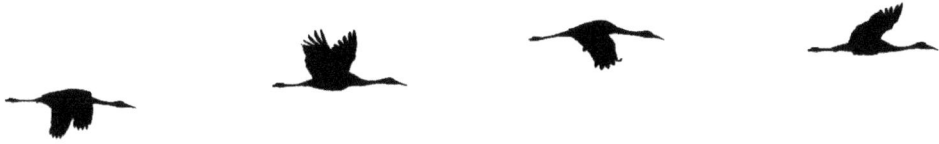

. . . a green which no artist could ever obtain on his palette, a green of which neither the varied tints of vegetation nor the shades of the most limpid sea could ever produce the like! If there is a green in Paradise, it cannot be but of this shade, which most surely is the true green of Hope.

Jules Verne, Le Rayon Vert, 1882
words found on March 27, 2012

9 781937 002695